BIG
RED
DIARY
2020

PLUTO PRESS

First published 2019 by Pluto Press
345 Archway Road, London N6 5AA

www.plutobooks.com

Copyright © Pluto Press 2019

The right of the individual contributors to be identified as the authors of this work has
been asserted by them in accordance with the Copyright, Designs and Patents Act 1988

British Library Cataloguing in Publication Data
A catalogue record for this book is available from the British Library

ISBN 978 0 7453 4001 2

BIG RED DIARY 2020

Edited by Steve Platt

Designed by Tom Lynton

Picture Research by Izzy Koksal

Writers: Brekhna Aftab, David Castle, Katherine Connelly, Marc Hudson, Silveried McKenzie, Tom Milson, Steve Platt, David Renton, Derek Wall

Photographs: Peter Arkell, Arpadi, Jean-Louis Atlan, Fibonacci Blue, Todd Buchanan, Biel Calderon, Howard Davies, Steve Eason, Johnny Eggitt, Melanie Friend, Robert Giroux, Global Justice Now, Francesco Gustincich, John Harris, Anders Hellberg, Jess Hurd, Timothy Krause, Kurdish struggles, David Mansell, Martin Mayer, Christine McIntosh, Igor Mukhin, Jeff Overs, PYMCA/UIG, Fabio Rodrigues, Ronald Reagan Library, Daniel Rosenthal, Ship to Gaza, Leif Skoogfors, Socialist Worker, Borja García de Sola Fernández, Christine Spengler, Julian Stallabrass, Hillel Steinberg, John Sturrock, Dora María Téllez, UN Climate change, Jose Villa

Welcome

From 1974 until 1987, Pluto Press published the Big Red Diary – annual pocket-sized diaries for activists, packed with political information and details of radical campaigns and organisations. Many of them were themed: there were diaries on feminism, disarmament, the politics of food and the politics of sport. To celebrate Pluto's 50th anniversary, we are publishing a new Big Red Diary for 2020. This diary looks back over 50 years of radical politics.

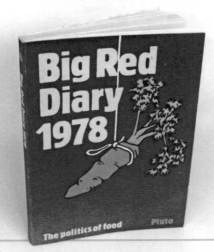

50 years of Pluto Press

Pluto Press was founded by Richard Kuper in 1969. It had its origins in the growing political consciousness and radical political activity of the late 1960s, which saw mass mobilisation against the Vietnam War, a radical student movement, the growth of second wave feminism and militant workers' organisations. Pluto was named after the Roman god; it is meant to convey the idea of the underworld answering back.

Pluto's output over the first few years was small – it was run part time by one person – and it didn't really gather momentum until 1972 when Richard Kuper was joined by Michael and Nina Kidron. Early successes included Sheila Rowbotham's *Hidden from History* and the *Big Red Diary*, which was published annually from 1974 until 1987. In its early years, Pluto published books and pamphlets for the organisation International Socialism (IS), but they parted company before the end of the 1970s, while IS transformed itself into the Socialist Workers Party.

Pluto's output grew and diversified through the 1980s, publishing the *State of the World* atlases, original

Pluto **A** Press
Workers' Handbook No.1

The Hazards of Work: How to Fight Them.

Physical Hazards / Patterns of Work
Chemical Hazards / Disease / Prevention
Accidents / Action / The Legal Machine
Safety Law / Winning Damages
Industrial Injury Benefits / Organising
Directory of Toxic Substances

Patrick Kinnersly

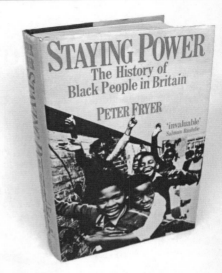

plays by authors such as Caryl Churchill and David Edgar, and crime fiction. It became a distributor for *Feminist Review*, *History Workshop* and others. But ultimately the political retreat and regressive economics of the 1980s caught up with it, and Pluto hit serious financial difficulties. Roger van Zwanenberg, co-founder of Zed Books, stepped in to become owner and managing director in 1987.

Roger, along with editorial director Anne Beech, rebuilt and refocused Pluto through the late 1980s and into the '90s. Out went the plays and fiction, but in came a more global perspective. Pluto became well known as a publisher of critical works on US foreign policy, especially as the UK publisher of the political writings of Noam Chomsky. It also published widely on Africa and the Middle East, and became the pre-eminent publisher of critical works on Israel and Palestine at a time when few other publishers would touch the subject.

Pluto's books were in much demand following the 2001 attacks on the Pentagon and World Trade Center, with Pluto having published two of the very few books available on Al Qaeda and the Taliban. With the Iraq war and occupation following, American imperialism and political Islam became central concerns of our publishing through the first decade of the 21st century. The 2000s also saw Pluto properly establish itself as an academic publisher, most notably through highly successful anthropology textbooks by Thomas Hylland Eriksen.

Roger van Zwanenberg retired in 2011 leaving Anne Beech as Managing Director. Recent years have seen Pluto build an online community around its website where it provides a platform for radical campaigns through podcasts, blogs and videos. With Veruschka Selbach appointed as Managing Director in 2017, Pluto's staff now sit on the board and own shares. Defying a harsh publishing and political climate, Pluto is currently growing, with staff in the US for the first time, and we look forward to another 50 years of independent radical publishing.

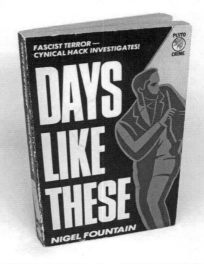

50 YEARS OF RADICAL POLITICS

The left

The story of the left since 1970 has been a series of attempts to sustain a mass movement beyond the Labour Party. Disenchantment was already widespread under Harold Wilson, with radical criticism of the party from a range of sources, including the trade union, anti-war and women's movements.

The Communist Party had 30,000 members at the start of the 1970s. However, the suppression of human rights, and particularly sending Soviet tanks to Hungary in 1956 and Czechoslovakia in 1968, had discredited the USSR as a model for younger socialists. The largest Trotskyist party of the 1960s, Gerry Healy's Socialist Labour League (later renamed the Workers' Revolutionary Party), also had limited appeal due to a top-down, bullying leadership.

Other groups seemed livelier, including the International Marxist Group and the International Socialists. The IMG, although never having more than about 1,000 members, was central to protests against the Vietnam war. The International Socialists reached a peak of around 5,000 members in the mid-1970s. It contributed to the 1970s' workers' movement, and then (renamed the Socialist Workers Party) to anti-fascism through the Anti-Nazi League.

In the mid-1980s, a new generation of socialists was shaped by hostility to Thatcherism and the passivity of Neil Kinnock's Labour. Some sought a base in local government, including Ken Livingstone in London and Militant in Liverpool. Other traditions foundered: the IMG dissolved itself to join Labour, the Communist Party dissolved following the collapse of the Soviet Union.

Militant's expulsion from Labour led the group to seek alliances with others on the left in the Socialist Alliance and Scottish Socialist Party. Six members of the SSP were elected to the

Scottish Parliament in 2003.

The 2003 war in Iraq was met with huge protests. Having launched the Stop the War coalition, the SWP joined the Socialist Alliance and then Respect – an alliance with former Labour MP George Galloway and others politicised by the Iraq War, including the Birmingham-based activist and councillor Salma Yaqoob. Galloway twice won seats in parliament under the Respect banner, but the alliance proved unsustainable and his radical image had already been shredded long before the time he gave his backing to Nigel Farage's Brexit party in 2019.

Several left parties fell apart due to sexual politics. The WRP collapsed after Gerry Healy was accused of the systematic abuse and rape of young women members. The SSP was dissolved after its best-known member and MSP, Tommy Sheridan, sued to silence press reports of alleged visits to swingers' clubs. Several hundred SWP members left in 2012–13, after accusations of rape and sexual harassment against its former national secretary.

Although not avowedly socialist, the Greens have adopted many left-wing policies and enjoyed significant electoral success, including the election of former leader Caroline Lucas as MP in 2010 and 274 local councillors in 2019. The Scottish Greens currently have six seats in the Scottish Parliament.

Since 2015, most socialist activists' hopes have returned to the Labour Party. Jeremy Corbyn's strategy of using social movements to balance against the Labour right has enthused many on the left. It remains to be seen whether the forces that his election as Labour leader mobilised can hold together in the face of internal divisions or the external pressures unleashed by Brexit.

50 YEARS OF RADICAL POLITICS

Social issues

Social movements have addressed oppressive and unequal situations across a wide range of issues, far beyond the traditional left concern of workplace pay and conditions. They have drawn in activists from diverse political and economic backgrounds who have been politicised around particular issues. Central issues of concern in the UK have been housing, healthcare and education.

Access to adequate housing became an accepted principle of the British welfare state. But some groups, including migrants, single people and even homeless families remained excluded. A huge squatting movement in the 1970–80s involved up to 50,000 people at its peak, and local councils were given a statutory duty to house certain categories of homeless in 1977.

The Thatcher government began a radical attack on social housing, however, ending almost all new council building and introducing the 'right to buy' for existing tenants. Private sector deregulation resulted in short-term tenancies and greatly increased rents, as well as the sort of lax building standards that led to the Grenfell Tower fire, which killed 72 people in 2017. Housing campaign networks and renters' unions have emerged around the country in response, challenging the perception of housing as profit-making assets rather than a fundamental right.

The commodification of healthcare similarly accelerated in the 1980s, and continues to this day. In 1983, the Conservative government published the Griffiths Report, which argued for 'modern management practices' in the NHS. Wholesale privatisation was ruled out because the NHS was seen as politically untouchable. Nevertheless, the National Health Service and Community Care Act 1990 introduced an 'internal market', resulting in hospitals that have become fragmented into autonomous, competing entities forced to prioritise balancing books and meeting targets rather than quality of care.

The Health and Social Care Act 2012 marked a further critical turning point towards privatisation, increasing the private income hospitals can earn from 2% to 49%. Thousands rallied against the bill in 2012, just as tens of thousands rallied in 2018 to oppose further cuts. In 2016, junior doctors participated in a general strike over contractual terms. Meanwhile, the Immigration Act 2014 imposed ID checks on patients, forcing migrants to prove their eligibility for treatment and charging up front for care. Campaigns have emerged to challenge the extension of border logic to health.

In education, over 50,000 protested in 2010, against proposed increases in university tuition fees and cuts to teaching budgets. These were introduced in 2012 and by 2017, student debt had soared to over £100 billion.

Protests around social issues have sometimes proven highly effective at targeting specific policies. 2020 marks the 30th anniversary of the poll tax rebellion – a movement of millions whose refusal to pay a regressive tax brought down Thatcher after eleven years of hard-line rule. The Wages for Housework campaign of the 1970s continues to galvanise struggles against the devaluation of women's work. More recently, the anti-austerity Spanish *indignados* movement in 2011 sparked the Occupy movement, while Mexico's Zapatistas and Brazil's Landless Workers' Movement have brought indigenous struggles to the fore. These movements continue to inspire alternatives to capitalism's organisation of social relations.

50 YEARS OF RADICAL POLITICS

Trade unions

The 1970s was a dynamic period for trade union activity in Britain. Union membership had experienced healthy growth after the Second World War and peaked at 13 million in 1979.

In 1972, miners went on strike for the first time in 46 years. The Conservative government declared a state of emergency, imposed a three-day week and then lost a general election. The incoming Labour government negotiated a deal with the strikers. During the early 1970s, it passed various laws enhancing workers' rights and social benefits as part of a 'social contract' that required pay restraint by the unions.

However, increasing inflation due to the 1973 oil crisis, industrial decline and balance of trade difficulties led to deteriorating industrial relations, union demands for higher wages and better working conditions culminated in widespread strikes during the so-called 'Winter of Discontent' in 1978–79.

The Labour government lost credibility, leading to Margaret Thatcher's election in 1979. Anti-trade unions laws, the privatisation of nationalised industries and high unemployment undermined union power. The miners again took action in the year-long 1984–85 strike against pit closures. This time they were defeated, marking the demise of extensive union action and influence.

The rights we enjoy as workers in Britain today are the result of over a century of collective struggle. But inequality remains rampant and executive pay has risen out of all proportion to that of ordinary workers. Today, after three decades of decline, some unions are again experiencing a limited growth in members, particularly in the private sector. However, the regeneration of a robust workers' movement remains partial and uncertain.

Democratic/civil rights

Democratic rights have been fiercely contested over the past 50 years. Joining what became the European Union made Brussels-crafted laws binding on the UK. This gave rise to mounting resentment, exacerbated by the democratic deficit of the union. However, Britain's accession also paved the way for changes to UK law that better protect human rights, such as around data protection, equal pay, employment and disability.

In the 1960s, the Northern Ireland civil rights movement came together to combat systematic anti-Catholic discrimination and violence. With the police and other arms of the state siding with the Protestant Unionists, this battle for civil rights escalated into decades of violence, claiming over 3,500 lives. In 1998, a peace agreement was struck that established a power-sharing government between Unionists and nationalists.

Arguments for self-determination and greater autonomy gained force during 18 years of Conservative rule from 1979. The 1997 Labour government created a devolved Scottish parliament and Welsh assembly. In Scotland, demands for full independence were defeated in the 2014 referendum, but Brexit – which Scotland voted heavily against – led to increased pressure to revisit the issue.

A number of attempts have been made to change the way MPs are elected. In 2011, the coalition government held a referendum on a form of partially proportional representation; the proposal was rejected and the 'first-past-the-post' voting system continues. In 1999, the Labour government drastically reduced the number of House of Lords peers who inherited their seats, and in 2005 it created the Supreme Court to replace the House of Lords as the court of last resort. The House of Lords remains wholly unelected.

50 YEARS OF RADICAL POLITICS

Anti-war and peace

Since 1945, the dominant expression of British imperialism has been its 'special relationship' with the US. It was dealt an important blow in the 1960s when Labour's Harold Wilson declined to commit British troops to the war in Vietnam. Anti-war feeling was expressed on the streets. In March 1968, the Vietnam Solidarity Campaign marched on the US embassy in Grosvenor Square; 100,000 demonstrated in October. A further demonstration took place the following October in solidarity with the huge Moratorium to End the War in Vietnam protests in the US.

Margaret Thatcher's vociferous support for the US in the Cold War, extending to the stationing of American cruise missiles in Britain, galvanised anti-nuclear and peace activists. For 19 years from 1981, women activists ran a peace camp at RAF Greenham Common. In October 1983, the Campaign for Nuclear Disarmament (CND), a powerful campaigning force against nuclear weapons in the 1950s–60s, organised a demonstration of hundreds of thousands – co-ordinated with others across Europe.

Tony Blair's support for the US-led 'war on terror' provoked the creation of an unparalleled anti-war movement. The Stop the War coalition organised, alongside the Muslim Association of Britain and CND, the largest demonstration in British history in February 2003, when between one and two million marched against war on Iraq. Millions more marched worldwide. Blair's premiership never recovered; he resigned in 2007. Longstanding anti-war campaigner Jeremy Corbyn overwhelmingly won the 2015 Labour leadership contest. Stop the War and other groups continue to mobilise against Britain's wars. With Donald Trump in the White House, the anti-war and peace movements remain vitally important.

50 YEARS OF RADICAL POLITICS

The green movement

The modern green movement emerged in the late 1960s/early 1970s. Atmospheric nuclear tests raised concern and scientific reports such as *The Limits to Growth* suggested that environmental problems threatened both humanity and the rest of nature.

Friends of the Earth, Greenpeace and other NGOs campaigned to 'save the whale' and halt pollution, and were soon joined by Green parties. By the late 1970s, most western European countries had Ecology or Green parties, with the anti-nuclear power movement stimulating growth. In 1983, the German Greens entered the then West German parliament.

During the 1990s, more radical direct-action movements became significant with campaigners setting up protest camps and disrupting road construction in the UK. The green movement became truly international in the 21st century with Green parties established in countries as diverse as the Philippines and Chile. Grassroots green activism has spread and individuals such as Berta Cáceres from Honduras have been assassinated by powerful forces threatened by their campaigns for environmental justice.

Green lifestyles have also influenced the movement; animal rights concerns have fed into the green movement and today veganism is growing fast. Increasingly, climate change has become the number one issue for greens. While mainstream politicians and the media have promoted renewable energy, direct action networks such as Extinction Rebellion have called for more radical action. Disruptive protest, local campaigns against fracking and parliamentary politics are just some of the aspects of the green movement today.

50 YEARS OF RADICAL POLITICS

International solidarity

Many forms of solidarity – taking action to support others in their struggles for justice – have sprung up in the past 50 years. People with particular skills have worked in majority world countries, providing basic services and training local people. Examples include medical efforts in El Salvador and Nicaragua during the Reagan-backed wars, and the foundation of Médecins Sans Frontières and spin-offs such as Engineers without Borders. Such efforts can require working relationships with questionable governments, sometimes forcing charities into silence on the causes of problems they seek to resolve.

Less institutionalised solidarity efforts have included convoys to Bosnia, medical aid to Iraq during the sanctions between the Gulf wars, the 'human shield' efforts in the same countries, the international solidarity movement in Palestine and the sanctuary movement in the US. Even more directly, some have fought in Rojava, northern Syria, alongside the Kurds.

Indirect forms of solidarity include pressuring governments to change policies – to increase aid budgets or impose sanctions on regimes such as apartheid South Africa. Efforts to raise awareness of problems and funds for their amelioration – often involving celebrities and moments of collective public virtue, such as the 1985 Live Aid concerts and the Comic Relief Red Nose campaigns, have become a staple of the charity-industrial complex.

Solidarity is driven by the best of human impulses – the desire to help, to overcome injustice or to make the world better. That said, it can be subject to abuses of power and privilege, slip into 'white saviour complex' models of thought or behaviour, or result in more local injustices being overlooked or ignored.

50 YEARS OF
RADICAL POLITICS

Global justice

Described as 'the movement of movements', the one for global justice includes NGOs, protest groups and radical networks. It links campaigns against neoliberal globalisation with those for environment protection, peace, LGBTIQ+ equality and much else.

It might be argued that the movement as we know it today was born in November 1999, when around 70,000 people protested at a meeting of the World Trade Organisation in Seattle. However, it has existed in some form for decades. 'Fair trade' started with solidarity buying of coffee from Angola and Nicaragua and is today a massive commercial force. Activism around AIDS and HIV in the USA during the 1980s morphed into a global call to pressure pharmaceutical companies to allow the production of cheaper generic drugs to help sufferers in Africa.

During the 1990s, Mexico's Zapatistas used international meetings, or 'encuentros', to bring together radical environmentalists, workers, anarchists and campaigners for fair trade. The world wide web allowed national campaigns to become global. Increasingly, activists in one part of the globe can work directly with those in another.

During the early years of the 21st century, huge demonstrations were held at meetings of organisations such as the International Monetary Fund and World Bank, opposing economic policies that impoverished the poor and enriched corporations. Via Campesina, a global network of peasant farmers, whose slogan is 'Globalising hope, globalising the struggle', is a leading part of the 21st-century movement. Today, from opposing sweatshop labour to fighting for food sovereignty, the global justice movement remains diverse and dynamic.

50 YEARS OF RADICAL POLITICS

Anti-racism

Despite the 1965 Racial Equality Act, discrimination and prejudice remained widespread in the UK into the 1970s. Successive amendments to the Act sought to promote racial equality, with some success, and great advances were made through grassroots organisation and campaigning.

BAME (black and minority ethnic) workers were often at the forefront of labour activism, with South Asian workers leading the two-year Grunwick strike in 1976–78. Organisations such as the Indian Workers' Association and Southall Black Sisters were among the first to build inter-community solidarity and tackle intra-community issues. In London's East End, Bengali youth movements played a major role in driving racist organisations from the streets following the murder of Altab Ali in 1978. Community defence organisations such as the Newham Monitoring Project were set up to provide support against discrimination, violence and police misconduct. The 1987 election produced the first black MPs in the modern era, including Diane Abbott. BAME representation in the current parliament has increased to 51.

Despite changing social attitudes, structural inequality remained. Police harassment and high unemployment triggered riots in a number of cities. The MacPherson inquiry into the 1993 racist murder of Stephen Lawrence detailed institutional racism in the Metropolitan Police.

More recently, the rise in racist, Islamophobic, and antisemitic violence highlights the challenges ahead. At state level, Theresa May's 'hostile environment' for immigrants, the Windrush scandal, deportations and the political climate around Brexit have all led to new organisations and forms of anti-racist resistance.

Anti-fascism

The highpoint of post-war anti-fascism occurred between 1976 and 1982. Operating in unfavourable circumstances – as James Callaghan's Labour government turned towards neoliberalism, paving the way for Thatcher – Rock Against Racism and the Anti-Nazi League (ANL) won the support of musicians, writers and photographers, developed a critique of institutional anti-racism pioneered by black radicals, and mobilised hundreds of thousands of people to defeat the fascists of the National Front.

Following the ANL's demise in 1982, groups such as Red Action and then Anti-Fascist Action harried the far right, forcing it to rebuild on largely electoral lines, notably through the British National Party, which elected its first councillor in 1993.

At the start of the 1990s, the Anti-Nazi League was relaunched; the ANL and its successors (presently Stand Up to Racism) have maintained the campaign's alliance of Trotskyists and Labour left without the excitement of the original. The anti-fascist research group and magazine, *Searchlight* – part of the original ANL – broke from United Against Fascism in the early 2000s and then, following a split of its own, gave birth to today's campaign, Hope not Hate.

The far right today is different from its predecessors. It is less dependent on the model of the interwar fascist parties and motivated by anti-Muslim rather than anti-black racism. It is boosted by the centre right's turn to racial exclusion, and by the space the far right has established online and internationally.

As memories of interwar European fascism and the Nazis fade, and the new far right takes on new forms, the work of anti-fascism is becoming more difficult. The essential task remains the same, however: to isolate the hard right from its more equivocal allies.

50 YEARS OF RADICAL POLITICS

LGBTQ+

The past 50 years have seen dramatic changes for the LGBTQ+ community in the UK – from the decriminalisation of sex between men to lifting the ban on openly gay military personnel, equalising the age of consent, revoking Section 28 of the Local Government Act 1988 (which forbade schools from portraying the 'acceptability of homosexuality as a pretended family relationship'), marriage equality and the largest number of LGBTQ+ parliamentarians in the world.

The community reckoned with the deadly *Admiral Duncan* pub bombing of 1999, battled against stigma and demonisation in the HIV/AIDS epidemic, and has continued to fight everyday discrimination. The growth of Pride celebrations across the country is testament to the ever-increasing visibility of the LGBTQ+ community; they remain crucial as gender non-conforming identities and transgender activism enter into the public discourse.

Most recently, action has ranged from campaigns for changes to outdated laws and regulations on issues such as blood donation to the continuing struggle for transgender rights and visibility in the face of hostile media representation. With new-found legal freedoms and growing tolerance and acceptance of deviant identities, the community has also had to come to terms with the rise of phenomena such as the 'pink pound' and the sponsoring of events such as Pride by multinational corporations, causing a reckoning with the radical history of such events.

The mainstreaming of previously subversive elements of the LGBTQ+ scene, from drag to gay clubbing, has resulted in far-reaching debate over how the community can protect its heritage while ensuring that LGBTQ+ people can achieve representation, equality and acceptance.

50 YEARS OF RADICAL POLITICS

Feminism

The radicalism of the 1960s had far-reaching implications for women. In 1968, a strike of women machinists at Ford provided the momentum for the 1970 Equal Pay Act.

The UK's first women's liberation conference was organised in 1970, marking the beginning of 'second wave' feminism. Its initial demands were free abortion and contraception, equal opportunities, free nurseries and equal pay. High-profile protests included the 1971 picket of the Miss World contest.

The movement was characterised by debates between socialist feminists, who saw women's oppression as a mechanism of capitalist society that could be collectively challenged by working-class women and men, and radical, separatist feminists, who saw women's oppression as a product of a patriarchal society and thus counterposed the interests of all women to common class interests. Radical feminism increasingly dominated, which resulted in a shift in focus onto violence against women – initiating, for example, Reclaim the Night.

'Third wave' feminism, originating in the 1990s, was not a self-defined movement and some claim that around 2008 it was supplanted by a 'fourth wave'. It emphasised personal choice and the media happily played along with the idea that feminism equated to individual advancement. These waves also championed intersectionality, understanding women's oppression as one feature of a wider oppressive system.

Today, the language of feminism is espoused by corporations and warmongers. But it also inspires marchers against Donald Trump and those resisting austerity, which has proved devastating to the lives of working women. A new wave faces a stark choice.

30 MONDAY

31 TUESDAY

A police raid on the **STONEWALL INN** gay bar in New York's Greenwich Village prompts six days of unprecedented resistance from patrons and local residents. Exasperated by years of legal oppression, discrimination and violence (New York even has a statute enforcing 'gender appropriate' clothing), the LGBT community finally snaps and fights back against the police. The 'Stonewall riots' act as a catalyst for a new, militant 'gay liberation' movement demanding equal rights. On 26 June 2015, two days before the anniversary of Stonewall, the US supreme court finally rules 5-4 in favour of same-sex marriage nationwide.

EAST VILLAGE

LESBIAN & GAY NEIGHBORS

1969

1 WEDNESDAY

New Year's Day
Bank/federal holiday (UK and US)

ON THIS DAY 1959
Cuban dictator Fulgencio Batista flees the island
in the face of revolution led by Fidel Castro

2 THURSDAY

Bank holiday (Scotland)

3 FRIDAY

ON THIS DAY 1792
Mary Wollstonecraft completes *A Vindication
of the Rights of Woman*

4 SATURDAY

ON THIS DAY 1901
The writer, historian and activist CLR James
is born in Tunapuna, Trinidad

5 SUNDAY

6 MONDAY

ON THIS DAY 1977
EMI drops the Sex Pistols punk-rock
band due to 'adverse publicity'

7 TUESDAY

8 WEDNESDAY

ON THIS DAY 1642
Galileo Galilei dies under house arrest, nine years after
facing the Roman Inquisition on heresy charges

9 THURSDAY

10 FRIDAY

ON THIS DAY 1981
The Farabundo Marti National Liberation Front (FMLN)
launches a general offensive in El Salvador

1970

Four unarmed students are killed and another nine wounded at **KENT STATE UNIVERSITY** on 4 May when the Ohio National Guard opens fire during protests against US-backed ground incursions and bombing of Cambodia. Other students are shot in the coming weeks, including two deaths at Jackson State College, Mississippi, as protests spread against the extension of the war in Vietnam. More than four million students join a nationwide strike. In December, Congress bars US ground forces from future military action in Cambodia and Laos. The air war continues unabated, however, until the eventual US defeat in south-east Asia in 1975.

11 SATURDAY

ON THIS DAY 1943
Carlo Tresca, prominent anarchist and US labour movement leader, is assassinated

12 SUNDAY

13 MONDAY

14 TUESDAY

ON THIS DAY 2011
Tunisian president Ben Ali flees to Saudi Arabia as 'Arab Spring' protests spread

The **BANGLADESH WAR OF INDEPENDENCE** culminates in defeat for the Pakistan army, after nine months of fighting. Originally included in the Pakistan state in the partition of India, East Pakistan soon comes into conflict with the government in the west over a range of economic, administrative and linguistic issues. With a military junta now in power in Pakistan, its refusal to recognise an overwhelming victory for the Awami League in the 1970 elections leads to a campaign of civil disobedience. The army engages in a vicious assault on the east, involving widespread killings and rapes. Aided by India, the Bangladesh independence movement is eventually victorious on 16 December.

1971

15 WEDNESDAY

ON THIS DAY 1919
German revolutionary leaders Rosa
Luxemburg and Karl Liebknecht are
murdered

16 THURSDAY

17 FRIDAY

ON THIS DAY 1991
The US-led 'Operation Desert Storm' begins
with a massive aerial bombardment in the
first Iraq war

18 SATURDAY

19 SUNDAY

ON THIS DAY 1929
Trotsky goes into exile from Stalinist Soviet Russia

20 MONDAY
Martin Luther King Day
Federal holiday (US)

ON THIS DAY 2009
A million people turn out for the
inauguration of Barack Obama as the first
African-American president of the US

21 TUESDAY

22 WEDNESDAY

ON THIS DAY 1905
'Bloody Sunday' in St Petersburg as the Imperial Guard
fires on unarmed marchers heading to the Winter Palace
to present a petition to Tsar Nicholas II of Russia

23 THURSDAY

24 FRIDAY

1972

On 30 January, British troops open fire on unarmed protesters in Derry, Northern Ireland, during a demonstration against internment without trial. Fourteen people are killed and twelve wounded. The **BLOODY SUNDAY** shootings are one of the worst incidents in the 30-year conflict known as The Troubles, which claims more than 3,500 lives before the Good Friday peace agreement in 1998. One outcome of the agreement will be the Saville Inquiry into the Bloody Sunday shootings, which hears from 922 witnesses and exonerates the victims of persistent claims, by the British Army and state, challenging their innocence.

25 SATURDAY

Chinese New Year

ON THIS DAY 1981
Jiang Qing, widow of Mao Zedung, is given a death sentence, later commuted to life imprisonment, for 'counter-revolutionary crimes' in the Cultural Revolution

26 SUNDAY

Three years after a nationwide Women's Strike for Equality saw tens of thousands of women joining protests across the US, the supreme court rules in favour of a constitutional right to legal, safe abortion in the landmark **ROE V WADE** case.
The ruling is one of the high points of 'second-wave feminism', which grows rapidly in the late 1960s–1970s. The UK movement makes four core demands: equal pay now; equal education and job opportunities; free contraception and abortion on demand; and free 24-hour nurseries. The Sex Discrimination Act 1975, the first such legislation in the UK, outlaws discrimination based on sex or marital status in employment, education and the provision of goods, facilities and services.

27 MONDAY

ON THIS DAY 1945
The Soviet Red Army liberates the Auschwitz concentration camp, a year to the day after breaking the three-year siege of Leningrad

28 TUESDAY

29 WEDNESDAY

ON THIS DAY 1912
Anna LoPizzo is shot on the picket line during one of
the most famous strikes in American labour history,
following an attempt to cut wages in the textile mills

30 THURSDAY

ON THIS DAY 1948
Mohandas Gandhi is assassinated in New Delhi
by a right-wing Hindu nationalist

31 FRIDAY

ON THIS DAY 1980
Guatemalan police burn 39 people to
death in the Spanish embassy after its
occupation by indigenous peasants

1 SATURDAY

2 SUNDAY

ON THIS DAY 1972
The British embassy in Dublin is burnt down in
protests against the killing of 14 unarmed civilians
by British soldiers in Derry two days previously

3 **MONDAY**

4 **TUESDAY**

ON THIS DAY 1969
Al-Fatah leader Yasser Arafat is elected chairman
of the Palestine Liberation Organisation

5 **WEDNESDAY**

6 **THURSDAY**

ON THIS DAY 1918
The Representation of the People Act gets royal
assent, giving some women in the UK the right to
vote for the first time

7 **FRIDAY**

ON THIS DAY 1898
Emile Zola is tried for libel over his newspaper
editorial 'J'Accuse', exposing an army cover up
in the antisemitic Dreyfus affair

8 SATURDAY

9 SUNDAY

ON THIS DAY 1950
US senator Joe McCarthy starts his witch-hunt against alleged communists in a speech claiming that 200 State Department staff are Communist Party members

1974

The **'CARNATION REVOLUTION' IN PORTUGAL** overturns half a century of fascist rule and leads to the country's withdrawal from its overseas colonies. Starting as a peaceful coup led by mainly junior military officers in the Armed Forces Movement (MFA), it is joined by workers and other citizens, many of whom take direct control over their workplaces and public services. Portugal's first free elections take place on the anniversary of the coup on 25 April, which is declared a national holiday, Dia da Liberdade. The fall of the Portuguese dictatorship is quickly followed in 1975 by those in Spain and Greece, bringing democracy to the whole of western Europe for the first time.

1975

The capture of Saigon by North Vietnamese-led liberation forces on 30 April brings to an end to the **VIETNAM WAR**. The US mounts the largest ever helicopter evacuation as it withdraws its remaining military and civilian personnel in chaotic scenes that culminate in a desperate rush for the last helicopters to take off from the roof of the US embassy. Up to 1.5 million people die in Vietnam's war for independence, including 58,000 US military personnel. The war's aftermath includes the rise to power of the Pol Pot regime in neighbouring Cambodia, which murders upwards of a million people, a quarter of the population.

10 MONDAY

11 TUESDAY

ON THIS DAY 1990
Nelson Mandela is freed after 27 years in prison

12 WEDNESDAY

ON THIS DAY 1989
Belfast lawyer Pat Finucane is shot dead at dinner with his
wife and children by loyalist paramilitaries in collusion with
'rogue elements' in the Royal Ulster Constabulary

13 THURSDAY

14 FRIDAY

15 SATURDAY

ON THIS DAY 1999
Abdullah Ocalan, founder of the Kurdish liberation
party PKK, is captured in Nairobi and sentenced to
death (later commuted to life imprisonment) in Turkey

16 SUNDAY

ON THIS DAY 2005
The Kyoto Protocol comes into effect,
committing states to limit greenhouse gas
emissions to combat global warming

17 MONDAY

Presidents' Day
Federal holiday (US)

ON THIS DAY 1936
The Abortion Law Reform Association is formed in Britain
by socialists, suffragists and free-thinkers to fight the 1861
Offences Against the Person Act, which prescribes penalties
of life imprisonment for the 'crime' of abortion

18 TUESDAY

ON THIS DAY 2010
Wikileaks publishes the first of nearly 750,000
classified documents leaked by former US
army soldier Chelsea Manning

19 WEDNESDAY

20 THURSDAY

21 FRIDAY

ON THIS DAY 1848
The Communist Manifesto is published

A 'social contract' is in place between the UK Labour government and trade unions with a raft of positive legislation, food subsidies and rent control being offered in return for pay restraint. Trade unions have never been stronger (membership peaks at more than 12 million in 1980). They are also moving into new, previously unorganised sectors and taking on new, innovative forms of action. The two-year **GRUNWICK DISPUTE** for union recognition, involving mainly south Asian women workers, attracts widespread solidarity and mass pickets. Meanwhile, Lucas Aerospace shop stewards produce an alternative plan for socially useful production in the face of mass redundancies.

1976

22 SATURDAY

ON THIS DAY 1943
Three German student leaders of the 'White Rose' resistance movement are executed in Munich for high treason against Hitler's Third Reich

23 SUNDAY

ON THIS DAY 1848
French revolutionaries overthrow the Orleans monarchy and establish the Second Republic, in which socialist Louis Blanc attempts to establish workers' cooperatives

1977

Backed by prominent public figures in music, sport and the arts, as well as a broad coalition of political activists and trade unions (its 'big-name' supporters range from Brian Clough and Iris Murdoch to Melvyn Bragg and Neil Kinnock), the Anti-Nazi League is set up to oppose the rise of the far right in the UK. It organises counter-demonstrations against National Front marches and,

with **ROCK AGAINST RACISM** (RAR), two massive carnivals in 1978 involving bands such as The Clash, Steel Pulse and X-Ray Spex. RAR itself was set up at the end of 1976 in response to a drunken racist rant by Eric Clapton at a concert in Birmingham. Its rise coincides with the emergence of punk and the avowedly militant DIY ethos of the new music scene at the time.

24 MONDAY

ON THIS DAY 1895
Cuba's final War of Independence from Spain begins, planned in part by poet and revolutionary philosopher José Martí

25 TUESDAY

26 WEDNESDAY

27 THURSDAY

ON THIS DAY 1933
The Nazis set fire to the Reichstag, the German parliament, blaming communists

28 FRIDAY

29 SATURDAY

1 SUNDAY

St David's Day

ON THIS DAY 1869
Ethiopian fighters defeat Italian forces at the Battle of Adwa, securing Ethiopian sovereignty to become a symbol of African resistance against European colonialism

2 MONDAY

ON THIS DAY 2002
Workers assume control of the Zanon
tile factory in Argentina, establishing the
model of a 'factory without a boss'

3 TUESDAY

ON THIS DAY 1985
End of the year-long miners' strike against pit
closures, which began at Cortonwood colliery
in south Yorkshire, England, on 6 March 1984

4 WEDNESDAY

5 THURSDAY

ON THIS DAY 1955
The South African Congress of Trade
Unions (SACTU) is founded

6 FRIDAY

ON THIS DAY 1921
The leader of the Gold Coast's fight against British
imperialism, pan-Africanist Kwame Nkrumah, becomes
the first prime minister of independent Ghana

1978

A mounting campaign of civil disobedience, strikes and mass demonstrations during 1978–79 leads to the **OVERTHROW OF THE SHAH** in Iran and the eventual establishment of an Islamic republic. The rebellion against the shah, who is backed by the US and the west, involves trade unions, leftists and other secular forces. After the revolution, though, they are crushed by the Islamists, led by the returning Ayatollah Khomeini and the newly-formed Revolutionary (now Republican) Guard.

7 SATURDAY

ON THIS DAY 1921
At the Kronstadt naval base, Russia's Red Army attacks sailors, soldiers and civilians protesting widespread famine and the Bolshevik repression of strikes

8 SUNDAY

International Women's Day

ON THIS DAY 1914
International Women's Day, co-founded by German Marxist Clara Zetkin, is organised for the first time on what becomes a fixed annual date

MARCH

9 MONDAY

ON THIS DAY 1914
Emmeline Pankhurst is arrested under the Prisoners' Temporary Discharge Act, introduced to prevent Suffragette hunger strikers securing unconditional release; she will be imprisoned, released and rearrested ten times under the Act

10 TUESDAY

1979

The election victory of **MARGARET THATCHER**'s Conservative Party follows the 'winter of discontent', in which a series of strikes brings the trade union movement into direct conflict with the Labour government's policy of pay restraint. The election of Thatcher and that of Ronald Reagan as US president at the end of 1978 marks the end of the 'post-war consensus' and the rise of neoliberalism. Thatcher's government will bring in successive tranches of anti-union legislation, lay waste to British manufacturing industry, privatise large swathes of the public sector and liberalise the economy, while implementing large-scale cuts and reactionary social policies.

11 WEDNESDAY

ON THIS DAY 1987
Mikhail Gorbachev takes over as the youngest-ever general secretary of the Soviet Communist Party

12 THURSDAY

ON THIS DAY 1930
Mohandas Gandhi begins the Salt Satyagraha, challenging the British Raj

13 FRIDAY

ON THIS DAY 1979
Maurice Bishop's New Jewel Movement overthrows the Grenada government

14 SATURDAY

ON THIS DAY 1883
Karl Marx dies

15 SUNDAY

ON THIS DAY 1845
Friedrich Engels publishes *The Condition of the Working Class in England*

MARCH

16 MONDAY

ON THIS DAY 1968
Up to 500 unarmed villagers are murdered by US
troops in the My Lai massacre in Vietnam

17 TUESDAY

St Patrick's Day
Bank holiday (Northern Ireland)

ON THIS DAY 1921
Marie Stopes and Humphrey Verdon Roe
open the first birth control clinic in Britain

18 WEDNESDAY

ON THIS DAY 1834
Six farm workers from Tolpuddle, England,
are sentenced to penal transportation to
Australia for forming a trade union

19 THURSDAY

ON THIS DAY 1962
End of the Algerian War of Independence

20 FRIDAY

ON THIS DAY 2003
Beginning of the Iraq War

21 SATURDAY

ON THIS DAY 1960
South African police kill 69 protesters in
the Sharpeville massacre, forcing the
anti-apartheid movement underground

22 SUNDAY

1980

Robert Mugabe's Zimbabwe African National Union (ZANU) sweeps to power in the first elections after a protracted war of liberation against the country's white minority rulers. Zimbabwe, formerly known as Rhodesia, has been a British colony for 90 years. It has been ruled by Ian Smith's white segregationist government since a unilateral declaration of independence – not recognised internationally – in 1965. **ZIMBABWE'S LIBERATION** marks the end of Britain's last major colony and an empire that once spanned one quarter of the world.

The Irish republican hunger striker **BOBBY SANDS** dies in Northern Ireland's Maze prison a month after 30,000-plus votes gave him victory in a by-election to the British parliament. Two other prisoners, including another hunger striker, are elected in the Irish general election in June. The hunger strikes, in support of political status for IRA prisoners, result in ten deaths. They are met by intransigence by the Thatcher

government, but attract widespread support (100,000 people attend Sands' funeral) and are key to bringing about a shift towards a more political, rather than military, strategy by Sinn Fein and the republican movement.

1981

EVERYONE REPUBLICAN OR OTHERWISE HAS THEIR OWN PARTICULAR ROLE TO PLAY...

Bobby Sands MP

POET, GAEILGEOIR, REVOLUTIONARY, IRA VOLUNTEER

23 MONDAY

24 TUESDAY

ON THIS DAY 1980
Oscar Romero, archbishop of San Salvador and critic of the Salvadorean death squads, is assassinated while giving mass

25 WEDNESDAY

26 THURSDAY

27 FRIDAY

ON THIS DAY 1871
A revolutionary government is elected to run the
Paris Commune, but government troops bloodily
suppress the Communards by the end of May

28 SATURDAY

ON THIS DAY 1906
The Trades Disputes Act is introduced in the House
of Commons, completing 'the structure of modern
trade union liberties and bargaining strength'

29 SUNDAY

ON THIS DAY 1942
The Hukbalahap Philippine communist guerrilla
organisation is founded; its insurgency against
the government lasts five years

30 MONDAY

ON THIS DAY 1960
The African National Congress is banned as a state of emergency is declared in South Africa

31 TUESDAY

ON THIS DAY 1953
ONE, the first American magazine about homosexuality, begins publication

1 WEDNESDAY

ON THIS DAY 1649
Poor farmers begin digging plots at St George's Hill in Surrey, England, in one of the first acts of the Digger movement, which sought to set up egalitarian rural communities, sometimes occupying common land

2 THURSDAY

3 FRIDAY

ON THIS DAY 1895
Oscar Wilde goes on trial for homosexual activity and is imprisoned for two years

4 SATURDAY

Martin Luther King is assassinated

5 SUNDAY

'The Manifesto of the 343', signed by 343 women, who had secret abortions, including Simone de Beauvoir, demands that the French government legalise the procedure

1982

Thirty thousand women link hands in the 'Embrace the Base' protest action around RAF **GREENHAM COMMON** in southern England. Even bigger protests are seen the following year, when the largest ever demonstrations against nuclear weapons take place worldwide, including 600,000 in Germany and 250,000 in London. A peace camp set up at the base in 1981 in protest against plans to locate medium-range cruise missiles with nuclear warheads there, continues in various forms until 2000. Secret documents released years later reveal that the world had come within a matter of minutes of nuclear conflict between the Soviet Union and the west.

6 MONDAY

7 TUESDAY

ON THIS DAY 1803
Toussaint Louverture, leader of the Haitian
black slave revolution, dies in France

1983

Thomas Sankara, a Pan-Africanist military officer, comes to power as president of Upper Volta, which is renamed **BURKINA FASO** ('land of the upright people'). The 'democratic and popular revolution' makes great strides in infant mortality, education, the empowerment of women, anti-imperialism and even environmentalism. But economic problems and opposition to progressive social policies, both internally and externally, undermines the new government and Sankara is assassinated in 1987.

8 WEDNESDAY

ON THIS DAY 1950
Imprisoned for sedition, the revolutionary
Turkish poet Nazim Hikmet launches a hunger
strike for amnesty for political prisoners

9 THURSDAY

Passover

10 FRIDAY

Good Friday
Bank holiday (UK)

ON THIS DAY 1919
Emiliano Zapata, Mexican Revolution leader,
is assassinated by the government

11 SATURDAY

ON THIS DAY 1981
Riots last for three days in Brixton,
London, in response to racist policing

12 SUNDAY

Easter Sunday

13 MONDAY

Easter Monday, Vaisakhi (Sikh New Year)
Bank holiday (UK)

ON THIS DAY 1635
Fakhr al-Din, Druze independence leader
against the Ottoman Empire and Lebanon's
first freedom fighter, is executed

14 TUESDAY

ON THIS DAY 2002
Venezuelan president Hugo Chavez, who describes
his socialist movement as the 'Bolivarian
revolution', returns to power after being ousted
in a US-backed coup two days earlier

15 WEDNESDAY

16 THURSDAY

17 FRIDAY

A year-long **MINERS' STRIKE** against pit closures starts in Yorkshire in March. At the time, Britain has 174 working pits. Most are gone within a decade and the last deep mine closes in 2015. The Thatcher government uses every method at its disposal, including its new anti-union laws and unprecedented police mobilisation, to crush the resistance, which includes a nationwide miners' support movement. One of the key events is the 'Battle of Orgreave', when 6,000 police attack picketing miners. Afterwards 95 pickets are charged with riot and similar offences but all charges are thrown out or dropped and 39 later obtain compensation totalling £425,000.

1984

18 SATURDAY

Twenty-nine newly independent African and Asian countries meet at the Bandung Conference in Indonesia in a show of strength for the Non-Aligned Movement

19 SUNDAY

20 MONDAY

21 TUESDAY

Fresh from its defeat of the 1984–85 miners' strike, the Thatcher government turns to local council resistance to public spending cuts. Faced with **RATE-CAPPING** legislation prohibiting them from raising local taxes to maintain services, left-wing Labour councils refuse to set a budget for 1985–86 to try to force concessions. The last councils to sustain the fight are Lambeth and Liverpool, whose Militant-led councillors are denounced by Labour leader Neil Kinnock in a conference speech that plays a major part in the expulsion of what is deemed to be Militant's 'party within a party'. Further legislation in 1985 results in the abolition of the Ken Livingstone-led Greater London Council and other metropolitan authorities.

22 WEDNESDAY

ON THIS DAY 1526
The first New World slave revolt occurs in Haiti

23 THURSDAY

St George's Day

24 FRIDAY

Ramadan begins

ON THIS DAY 1916
Irish republicans mount an armed insurrection
against British rule in the Easter Rising

25 SATURDAY

ON THIS DAY 1974
Portuguese armed forces overthrow the ruling
Estado Novo dictatorship in what becomes
known as the Carnation Revolution, setting the
stage for colonies to achieve independence

26 SUNDAY

ON THIS DAY 1994
Nelson Mandela is elected president of South Africa

27 MONDAY

28 TUESDAY

ON THIS DAY 1967
Heavyweight champion boxer Muhammad Ali refuses induction into the US armed forces, leading to a charge for draft evasion and his being stripped of his titles

29 WEDNESDAY

ON THIS DAY 1992
Two days of rioting erupt in the aftermath of the Rodney King police brutality trial, leaving 38 dead, 1,500 injured and half a billion dollars in property damage in Los Angeles, California

30 THURSDAY

1 FRIDAY

International Workers' Day

ON THIS DAY 1949
Albert Einstein publishes 'Why Socialism' in the inaugural issue of *Monthly Review*

2 SATURDAY

ON THIS DAY 2003
Standing under a 'Mission Accomplished' banner on the *USS Lincoln* aircraft carrier, President George W Bush declares that 'major combat operations in Iraq have ended'

3 SUNDAY

ON THIS DAY 1968
French students protest the closure of the Sorbonne, setting off the May '68 wave of demonstrations and strikes by millions of students and workers

The Iran-Contra scandal, also known as **IRANGATE**, reveals that secret arms sales to Iran, which is subject to an arms embargo, are being made by the Reagan government to fund the Contra rebel movement in Nicaragua. The Sandinista National Liberation Movement overthrew the Somoza dictatorship in 1979 and had won national elections in 1984. A US-backed civil war was raging, however, and the Reagan administration was determined to bring a halt to the Sandinistas' revolutionary programme, which included widespread nationalisation and other socialist-oriented policies.

1986

4 MONDAY

At a rally for the eight-hour day at Haymarket Square in Chicago, a bomb is thrown at police; eight anarchists are later convicted of conspiracy and executed

5 TUESDAY

The **BLACK MONDAY** stock market crash on 19 October spreads worldwide over the next 24 hours in the worst single-day economic turmoil since 1929. Share prices tumble by almost a quarter in one day in the US and Canada, while those in Britain (26%), Spain (31%), Australia (42%) and Hong Kong (46%) are among other massive falls over the coming week or so. The crash is a foretaste of what is to come in 2007/08, although on this occasion the world economy eventually rides the storm, ushering in a sustained period of growth, albeit led by financialisation, over the coming decades.

1987

6 **WEDNESDAY**

7 **THURSDAY**

Vesak (Buddha Day)

ON THIS DAY 1429
The legend of Joan of Arc is born when she returns to the fray after seemingly being killed by an English arrow and inspires the French forces to break the siege of Orleans

8 **FRIDAY**

Bank holiday (UK)

ON THIS DAY 1945
VE (Victory in Europe) Day sees the unconditional surrender of Germany and the final defeat of the Nazi war machine

9 **SATURDAY**

ON THIS DAY 1960
The contraceptive pill is approved for use in the US

10 **SUNDAY**

ON THIS DAY 1857
Beginning of the mutiny against British rule in India

11 MONDAY

12 TUESDAY

ON THIS DAY 1916
The execution of James Connolly and
other leaders of the Easter Rising takes
place in Dublin

13 WEDNESDAY

14 THURSDAY

15 FRIDAY

ON THIS DAY 1381
Peasants' Revolt leader Wat Tyler is killed by
London's mayor during negotiations with
Richard II at Smithfield, London

'Children who need to be taught to respect traditional moral values are being taught that they have an inalienable right to be gay.' So says Prime Minister Margaret Thatcher at the 1987 Conservative Party conference. The following year her government introduces **SECTION 28** of the Local Government Act, which prohibits local authorities from 'promoting' homosexuality and ratchets up anti-gay prejudice in the wake of

the HIV/Aids epidemic then sweeping through gay communities. Section 28 galvanises the LGBT movement, however. Tens of thousands march in Manchester and London. Lesbian activists abseil into the House of Lords and protest live in the BBC *Six-o-Clock News* studio. The actor Ian McKellen comes out as gay to support protests, along with *EastEnders* star Michael Cashman, the first gay character in a British soap, who later helps set up the LGBT campaign group Stonewall.

1988

16 **SATURDAY**

17 **SUNDAY**

18 MONDAY

ON THIS DAY 1980
Citizens of Kwangju, South Korea, seize control of
their city, demanding democratisation, an end to
martial law and an increase in the minimum wage

19 TUESDAY

The **BERLIN WALL** comes down as the
Soviet bloc disintegrates across eastern
Europe. Most countries make relatively
peaceful transitions to new forms of
government, although in Romania the
autocratic Nicolae Ceauşescu clings
onto power until his execution with his
wife in December. The Soviet Union is
not officially dissolved until December
1991, by which time its twelve
constituent republics have all declared
independence. In China, meanwhile,
the world's biggest Communist Party
retains control with the crushing
of democratic opposition in the
Tiananmen Square massacre on 4 June.

1989

20 WEDNESDAY

21 THURSDAY

ON THIS DAY 1956
The first aerial test of the hydrogen bomb
renders Bikini Atoll uninhabitable

22 FRIDAY

23 SATURDAY

24 SUNDAY

Eid al-Fitr

ON THIS DAY 1798
The Society of United Irishmen, a republican
group influenced by the American and French
revolutions, rises up against English rule

1990

The repeal of the ban on the African National Congress (ANC) and release of its leader **NELSON MANDELA** after 27 years in prison sets in motion the end of apartheid following years of sanctions and cultural boycotts. Negotiations for the new multi-racial South Africa will take several years and when the first free elections finally take place in 1994 people queue for hours in the burning sun to cast their votes. A member of the South African Communist Party for most of his life, Mandela emphasised reconciliation and a broad coalition in government to build the new country.

25 MONDAY
Memorial Day, Federal holiday (US)
Spring bank holiday (UK)

26 TUESDAY

27 WEDNESDAY

ON THIS DAY 1871
The Paris Commune is crushed with 25,000 massacred

28 THURSDAY

29 FRIDAY

ON THIS DAY 1963
Peruvian revolutionary Hugo Blanco is captured after leading a 'Land or Death' peasant uprising that sparks the country's first agrarian reform

30 SATURDAY

31 SUNDAY

ON THIS DAY 1994
The US says it will no longer aim nuclear missiles at the former Soviet Union

1 MONDAY

2 TUESDAY

3 WEDNESDAY

4 THURSDAY

ON THIS DAY 1989
The Tiananmen Square massacre in Beijing
crushes pro-democracy protests in China

5 FRIDAY

World Environment Day

ON THIS DAY 2013
The Guardian publishes the first batch of
government documents leaked by US National
Security Agency whistle-blower Edward Snowden

6 SATURDAY

ON THIS DAY 1780
London's Newgate Prison is set ablaze during
the Gordon Riots

7 SUNDAY

ON THIS DAY 1903
James Connolly, who will later be executed for his
role in Ireland's Easter Rising, founds the Socialist
Labour Party with comrades in Edinburgh

Operation Desert Storm brings together
a US-led coalition of 38 nations in the
FIRST IRAQ WAR. After a massive
bombing campaign, mainly US and
UK land forces attack Iraq in response
to Iraqi dictator Saddam Hussein's
invasion of Kuwait. The war attracts
particular opposition for
the indiscriminate 'turkey
shoot' of an Iraqi column
of vehicles withdrawing from Kuwait.
It is the first major test of the 'new
world order' after the collapse of the
Soviet Union and for the philosophy of
humanitarian intervention advocated
by some sections of the left. A 'no fly'
zone guarantees Kurdish autonomy in
the north of Iraq but Saddam Hussein
will remain in power until the second
Iraq War in 2003.

1991

8 MONDAY

9 TUESDAY

1992

Three days of anti-immigrant rioting in the east German city of Rostock provide an early warning of the re-emerging **FAR-RIGHT THREAT** in post-Cold War Europe. A crowd of 3,000 applauds as neo-Nazis lead petrol bomb attacks on a shelter for asylum seekers. The police fail to stop them. Only a few people are ever convicted for the violence, and none for violence against the migrants. In the UK at the same time, the British National Party (BNP) is on the rise. It sets up the Combat 18 group, which takes its name from the first and eighth letters of the alphabet (AH, for Adolf Hitler) and is involved in attacks on the offices of the *Morning Star* and Democratic Left, among others.

10 WEDNESDAY

ON THIS DAY 1952
Trinidadian historian, novelist and critic CLR
James is detained at Ellis Island to await
deportation from the US

11 THURSDAY

12 FRIDAY

ON THIS DAY 1917
Hubert Harrison, a black intellectual and
labour leader, founds the Liberty League,
the first organisation of the 'New Negro
Movement'

13 SATURDAY

ON THIS DAY 1971
The *New York Times* publishes the Pentagon
Papers leaked by Daniel Ellsberg, proving that
the US government deliberately misled the
public over the Vietnam War

14 SUNDAY

ON THIS DAY 1983
Protests against General Pinochet, whose
military regime seized power in a murderous
coup ten years previously, bring 100,000
Chileans onto the streets

JUNE

15 MONDAY

Simon Bolivar issues his 'Decree of War to the Death' for independence from Spain in Venezuela

16 TUESDAY

Eugene Debs delivers an anti-war speech in Ohio for which he is tried for sedition; he runs for US president from jail and wins nearly a million votes

17 WEDNESDAY

China explodes the hydrogen bomb, joining the club of nuclear-armed states

18 THURSDAY

The 'Battle of Orgreave' sees an organised attack on picketing miners by thousands of police bussed in from around the country in a pivotal event of the 1984–85 UK miners' strike

19 FRIDAY

20 **SATURDAY**

World Refugee Day

21 **SUNDAY**

LA VIA CAMPESINA, an international movement of peasants, agricultural workers, rural women and indigenous communities, is founded to fight for local rights and food sovereignty in the face of increasing corporate control of agriculture. The movement, which now comprises almost 200 organisations in more than 80 countries, has battled against patent laws and seed monopolies, as well as violence against women. It campaigns for 'culturally appropriate' and sustainable agriculture and agrarian reform.

1993

JUNE

1994

Three thousand Zapatista Army of National Liberation insurgents seize towns and territory in Chiapas, Mexico, and issue their First Declaration and Revolutionary Laws. The announcement coincides with the North Atlantic Free Trade Agreement coming into effect and the **ZAPATISTAS** use the occasion to call for a wider revolt against neoliberalism. The Zapatistas' commitment to autonomous organisation and indigenous leadership, together with its broadly libertarian-socialist and environmentally-sustainable programme, attracts support across the world. They have since secured a high degree of self-government for Chiapas from the Mexican state.

22 MONDAY

ON THIS DAY 1955
Historian Eric Williams founds the People's National Movement, which later ushers in independence in Trinidad and Tobago

23 TUESDAY

ON THIS DAY 1937
George Orwell flees Spain

24 WEDNESDAY

ON THIS DAY 1901
Pablo Picasso's first exhibition opens in Paris,
where he is under police observation as a
suspected anarchist

25 THURSDAY

ON THIS DAY 1962
Mozambique's anti-colonial liberation party
FRELIMO is founded; in the early 1970s,
its guerrilla force of 7,000 fought 60,000
Portuguese colonial troops

26 FRIDAY

27 SATURDAY

28 SUNDAY

ON THIS DAY 1905
The Industrial Workers of the World
(Wobblies) trade union is founded in Chicago

29 **MONDAY**

30 **TUESDAY**

The first war on European soil since 1945 comes to an end after an estimated 100,000 deaths, up to 20,000 rapes and the displacement of more than two million people. The **BREAK-UP OF YUGOSLAVIA** in 1991 leads to a primarily three-way conflict between Serbs, Croats and Bosnian Muslims, with the Serbs in particular responsible for indiscriminate attacks on civilians, ethnic cleansing and other war crimes. A NATO bombing campaign during the summer of 1995 hits more than 300 Bosnian Serb targets, leading to a peace agreement later that year and Bosnian independence.

1995

1 WEDNESDAY

ON THIS DAY 1969
Nuclear non-proliferation treaty signed by the US,
USSR and 60 other countries

2 THURSDAY

ON THIS DAY 1809
Shawnee chief Tecumseh calls on all tribes
to unite against the encroachment of white
settlers on native land

3 FRIDAY

Federal holiday (US)

ON THIS DAY 1982
Black Panther and Move activist Mumia Abu-Jamal
is sentenced to death in the US

4 SATURDAY

Independence Day

ON THIS DAY 1920
'Only the little people pay taxes' – billionaire
property tycoon Leona Helmsley, the so-called
'Queen of Mean', was born on this day

5 SUNDAY

ON THIS DAY 1885
The Protect the King movement in Vietnam begins after
a French attack on the imperial capital of Hue, uniting
the country against French colonial rule

6 MONDAY

7 TUESDAY

8 WEDNESDAY

9 THURSDAY

ON THIS DAY 2005
Palestinian civil society launches a campaign for
boycott, divestment and sanctions (BDS) against Israel

10 FRIDAY

ON THIS DAY 1917
Emma Goldman is sentenced to two years in
jail for aiding draft resisters

11 SATURDAY

ON THIS DAY 1977
Gay News and its editor Denis Lemon are found guilty of blasphemous libel in the first case of its kind for more than 50 years, a private prosecution brought by anti-'porn' campaigner Mary Whitehouse

12 SUNDAY

Battle of the Boyne

ON THIS DAY 1985
The Live Aid concert for famine relief in Africa at London's Wembley Stadium is broadcast to 1.5 billion people in 160 countries

Following a couple of similar, smaller events in north London the previous summer, thousands of road protesters shut down the M41 in the west of the city in a mass street party. The party/protest is the most successful by the **RECLAIM THE STREETS** direct action group, which melds the burgeoning 'rave culture' and anti-roads protests of the early 1990s into an innovative and enjoyable form of political action. New criminal laws aimed at both protesters and ravers, passed in 1994, famously target music that 'includes sounds wholly or predominantly characterised by the emission of a succession of repetitive beats'.

1996

13 MONDAY

Bank holiday (Northern Ireland)

14 TUESDAY

ON THIS DAY 1789
The storming of the Bastille prison in Paris heralds the
French Revolution

15 WEDNESDAY

ON THIS DAY 1995
Up to 8,000 Muslim men are murdered by Serb forces
after being forced out of the UN-protected 'safe haven'
of Srebrenica in Bosnia

16 THURSDAY

17 FRIDAY

'Things can only get better', as Labour's election anthem has it. After 18 years of Tory rule, **TONY BLAIR'S NEW LABOUR** wins a landslide election victory with a 10% swing from the Conservatives and the largest number of seats (418 out of 659) the party has ever won. The large number of women MPs and a radical programme of devolution, the minimum wage and other social reforms creates a mood of great optimism across much of the left. But New Labour's commitment to deregulation and an essentially neoliberal economic programme is widely criticised and stores up huge problems for the future, even before the second Iraq war in 2003 turns out so catastrophically.

1997

18 **SATURDAY**

Nelson Mandela International Day

ON THIS DAY 1290
Every Jew in England is ordered out of the country by Edward I; more than 16,000 are forced to flee

19 **SUNDAY**

ON THIS DAY 1961
The Sandinista National Liberation Front (FSLN) is founded; in 1979 it will overthrow the Somoza dictatorship in Nicaragua

20 MONDAY

21 TUESDAY

Referendums on each side of the Irish border deliver an overwhelming endorsement of the **GOOD FRIDAY AGREEMENT**, bringing an end to 'the Troubles' in Northern Ireland after 30 years of conflict and some 3,000 deaths. The agreement is based on the fundamental principle of no change in the status of the North without democratic consent and marks the end of the IRA's armed struggle against British rule. All the main paramilitary groups agree to decommission their weapons and new institutions of devolved government, power sharing and cross-border cooperation are put in place. Gerry Adams, president of the IRA's political wing, Sinn Fein, acknowledges the remaining gulf between republican and unionist communities, which he says 'must be bridged on the basis of equality'.

1998

22 WEDNESDAY

23 THURSDAY

ON THIS DAY 1900
W E B Du Bois attends the first Pan African Conference in
London, where he makes the statement later immortalised
in his 1903 book *Souls of Black Folk*: 'The problem of the
20th century is the problem of the colour-line'

24 FRIDAY

25 SATURDAY

ON THIS DAY 1846
Henry David Thoreau is jailed for refusing to
pay taxes due to his opposition to slavery and
the Mexican-American war

26 SUNDAY

ON THIS DAY 1956
Gamal Abdel Nasser, president of Egypt,
announces the nationalisation of the Suez Canal

27 MONDAY

ON THIS DAY 1972
Selma James and Mariarosa Dalla Costa publish
*The Power of Women and the Subversion of the
Community*, which identifies women's unwaged care
work as an essential element of capitalism

28 TUESDAY

ON THIS DAY 1957
The Situationist International is founded in Italy

29 WEDNESDAY

30 THURSDAY

ON THIS DAY 1935
The first Penguin paperbacks are published,
including *A Farewell to Arms* by Ernest Hemingway,
revolutionising book publishing

31 FRIDAY
Eid al-Adha

1 SATURDAY

ON THIS DAY 1833
The Slavery Abolition Act comes into effect,
abolishing slavery in the British empire

2 SUNDAY

ON THIS DAY 1980
A bomb at Bologna's railway station, attributed
to neo-fascists as part of the so-called 'strategy of
tension', kills 85 and injures more than 200

The **'BATTLE OF SEATTLE'** greets the
World Trade Organisation ministerial
conference on 30 November. The
'carnival against capitalism' brings tens
of thousands of demonstrators onto
the streets in the biggest protest to
date against neoliberal globalisation.
Those involved range from trade
unions, environmental organisations
and the Jubilee 2000 anti-debt
campaign to traditional left groups
and anarchist 'black bloc' protesters.
The Seattle police chief is to resign
over his response to the protest and
in 2007 a federal jury rules that the
police had violated demonstrators'
rights by arresting and detaining
them without due cause.

1999

3 MONDAY

Bank holiday (Scotland)

4 TUESDAY

ON THIS DAY 1983
The Marxist pan-Africanist Thomas Sankara assumes
power in Burkina Faso

5 WEDNESDAY

6 THURSDAY

ON THIS DAY 1945
The US drops the atomic bomb on Hiroshima

7 FRIDAY

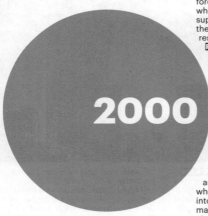

2000

Israel withdraws its military forces from southern Lebanon, which it first occupied with the support of Christian militias in the Lebanon war of 1982. The war resulted in the forced exile of the **PALESTINE LIBERATION ORGANISATION** from Lebanon and massacres by Israeli allies at the Sabra and Shatila refugee camps. The South Lebanon Security Belt, set up in 1985, was intended to provide a buffer zone between Lebanon and northern Israel but it became a target for resistance, primarily by Hezbollah fighters. Clashes continue between Hezbollah and Israel, including in 2006, when a Hezbollah incursion into northern Israel prompts a massive Israeli bombardment and air attacks. Israeli troops again invade and temporarily occupy southern Lebanon.

8 SATURDAY

ON THIS DAY 1974
US president Richard Nixon announces his resignation in the face of threatened impeachment

9 SUNDAY

ON THIS DAY 1650
Parliament passes an Act outlawing 'blasphemous' sects like the Ranters, one of the most radical to emerge during the English Revolution, which denies the authority of churches and priests

2001

The 11 September **ATTACKS ON NEW YORK AND WASHINGTON** are met with US president George W Bush's declaration of a global 'war on terror'. It begins with the invasion of Afghanistan on 7 October. The invasion is intended to crush the al-Qaeda terror group and remove the Islamist Taliban regime. Some al-Qaeda fighters escape, however, including its leader Osama bin Laden, who is finally located and killed in Pakistan ten years later. Lasting military success in Afghanistan proves even more elusive and the ill-defined and often indiscriminate 'war on terror' is similarly ineffective as more countries become targets of Islamist terror attacks.

10 MONDAY

11 TUESDAY

ON THIS DAY 1961
The Berlin Wall is completed,
escalating Cold War tensions

12 WEDNESDAY

ON THIS DAY 2017
Anti-fascist protester Heather Heyer is killed when a
vehicle is driven into people at a white supremacist
'Unite the Right' gathering in Charlottesville, Virginia

13 THURSDAY

14 FRIDAY

ON THIS DAY 1842
The Seminole Native American tribe is forced to
begin the Long March to Oklahoma after defeat
by the US army in Florida

15 SATURDAY

ON THIS DAY 1947
India becomes independent after 200 years
of British rule

16 SUNDAY

ON THIS DAY 1819
Mounted soldiers attack a 60,000-strong crowd rallying for
parliamentary reform in Manchester, northern England, in
what becomes known as the Peterloo Massacre

17 MONDAY

18 TUESDAY

19 WEDNESDAY

ON THIS DAY 1953
Mohammad Mossadegh, the popular democratically-elected prime minister of Iran, is overthrown by a CIA-backed coup

20 THURSDAY

Islamic New Year (1442 AH)

ON THIS DAY 1968
The Soviet army invades Czechoslovakia, ending the 'Prague Spring'

21 FRIDAY

ON THIS DAY 1940
Leon Trotsky is murdered by a Stalinist agent in Mexico

22 SATURDAY

Chelsea Manning is sentenced to 35 years in prison for passing more than 700,000 government files to WikiLeaks

23 SUNDAY

The Italian-born anarchists Nicola Sacco and Bartolomeo Vanzetti are executed after being wrongfully convicted for robbery and murder

The **WORLD SOCIAL FORUM** brings together social movements from across the globe in Porto Alegre, Brazil, in the first of what is to become an annual gathering. Organising under the slogan 'Another World is Possible', the forum describes itself as 'plural, diverse, non-governmental and non-partisan'. It provides a focus for the global justice movement, offering 'a permanent space and process to build alternatives to neoliberalism'. Usually timed to coincide with the World Economic Forum's annual meetings in Davos, Switzerland, its most recent gathering, also in Brazil, attracts representatives from 120 countries. Along with the first European Social Forum, held in the same year, the 2002 forum plays a major part in organising the global day of action against war on Iraq – said to be the biggest protest in world history – on 15 February 2003.

2003

Unprecedented worldwide protests, including a march variously estimated at between one and two million people in London, fail to stop the US-led **INVASION OF IRAQ**. US vice-president Dick Cheney says: 'My belief is we will, in fact, be greeted as liberators.' In the UK, a government-compiled 'dodgy dossier' claims that the Iraqi despot Saddam Hussein has developed weapons of mass destruction that are a mere 15-minute missile flight from British bases in Cyprus. No evidence for such weapons is ever found.

24 MONDAY

25 TUESDAY

ON THIS DAY 1968
Protests at the Democratic National Convention in Chicago are violently broken up by police, after which some of the organisers are charged with conspiracy to riot

26 WEDNESDAY

ON THIS DAY 1920
The 19th Amendment to the US Constitution is passed,
guaranteeing American women's right to vote

27 THURSDAY

28 FRIDAY

ON THIS DAY 1963
Martin Luther King makes his 'I have a dream' speech
to a huge civil rights rally in Washington DC

29 SATURDAY

ON THIS DAY 1533
Atahualpa, the last Incan emperor, is put to
death by the conquistador Pizarro

30 SUNDAY

ON THIS DAY 1980
The independent Solidarity trade union wins the
right to organise and strike in Poland

31 MONDAY

Bank holiday
(England, Wales, N Ireland)

ON THIS DAY 1944
The US Communist Party is formed in Chicago, Illinois

1 TUESDAY

2 WEDNESDAY

ON THIS DAY 1872
Russian revolutionary and anarchist theorist Mikhail Bakunin is expelled from the First International, presaging a split between the anarchist and Marxist factions of the workers' movement

3 THURSDAY

ON THIS DAY 2017
A protest camp becomes the largest gathering in Native American history after security guards for the Dakota Access Pipeline unleash dogs on indigenous water protectors near the Standing Rock Sioux tribal reservation in North Dakota

4 FRIDAY

ON THIS DAY 1970
The socialist Salvador Allende wins the presidential election in Chile

5 SATURDAY

ON THIS DAY 1877
Great Sioux chief Crazy Horse is killed by US soldiers

6 SUNDAY

ON THIS DAY 1960
The 'Manifesto of the 121' is signed by French
intellectuals, including Sartre, Blanchot and
others, supporting the right of Algerians to fight for
independence from the French

2004

In the same year that Mark Zuckerberg
founds Facebook with fellow students
at Harvard University (it will be another
three years before it is opened up to
non-students and begins its march
to world social media dominance),
internet 'hacktivism' takes off
through other channels, including
message boards such as 4chan.
Many of the early hacktivists
are left-libertarian or anarchist-
leaning, and the most famous
informal hacktivist collective,
Anonymous, targets government
agencies and corporations, as
well as child pornographers,
homophobes and Islamists,
among others. **ANONYMOUS**
also backs Wikileaks and the
Occupy movement, with
supporters wearing Guy
Fawkes masks as a striking
feature at a wide range
of protests.

7 MONDAY

Labor Day
Federal holiday (US)

ON THIS DAY 1901
The Boxer Rebellion ends with the Peace of Peking Treaty

8 TUESDAY

9 WEDNESDAY

ON THIS DAY 1869
Ali Ibn Muhammad, a leader of the Zanj uprising of
African slaves against the Abbasid Caliphate in Iraq,
begins freeing slaves and gaining adherents

10 THURSDAY

11 FRIDAY

ON THIS DAY 2001
Islamist terrorist attacks on New York City
and the Pentagon leave nearly 3,000 dead,
leading to the so-called 'war on terror'

The **KYOTO PROTOCOL** to the United Nations Framework Convention on Climate Change, committing states to reduce greenhouse emissions, comes into effect. A Global Day of Action is organised to coincide with the first UNFCCC meeting of the parties ('MOP1'). Demonstrations are held in at least 35 countries, with the number more than doubling in the third global day of action in 2007. Imaginative and eye-catching protests include the sculpting of a 15-ton polar bear from ice at Berlin's Brandenburg Gate, where it slowly melts.

12 SATURDAY

ON THIS DAY 1977
The journalist and Black Consciousness Movement activist Steve Biko is killed by state security officers in Pretoria, South Africa

13 SUNDAY

ON THIS DAY 1971
New York governor Nelson Rockefeller orders an attack on Attica Prison, which has been taken over by inmates following a prison riot

Photo © Greenpeace/ Daniel Rosenthal

14 MONDAY

ON THIS DAY 1791
Olympe de Gouges publishes the *Declaration of the Rights of Woman and the Female Citizen*, one of the first tracts to champion women's rights

15 TUESDAY

The election of Evo Morales and his Movement for Socialism in Bolivia sees a high point in the **'PINK TIDE'** in Latin America, following the elections of Hugo Chavez in Venezuela in 1999 and Luiz Inácio Lula da Silva (Lula) in Brazil in 2003. With a left-leaning government in power in Argentina and other victories including the election of Rafael Correa and his PAIS alliance in Ecuador in 2007, much of the international left looks to Latin America for hope and inspiration. Little more than a decade later, however, most of the left governments, mired in economic difficulties and corruption scandals, have been defeated in elections and the right is in the ascendancy.

2006

16 WEDNESDAY

ON THIS DAY 1973
Victor Jara, Chilean poet and songwriter, is tortured
and killed in Chile's national football stadium
following General Pinochet's coup against socialist
president Salvador Allende on 11 September

17 THURSDAY

ON THIS DAY 2011
The Occupy Wall Street protest camp against
economic inequality begins at Liberty
Plaza, Manhattan, under the slogan 'We
are the 99%'

18 FRIDAY

19 SATURDAY

Rosh Hashanah

ON THIS DAY 1955
Argentina ousts dictator Juan Perón

20 SUNDAY

ON THIS DAY 1907
Jacob Morenga, Namibia's first guerrilla leader,
is shot by British troops

21 MONDAY

ON THIS DAY 1956
Nicaraguan poet Rigoberto López Pérez assassinates
Anastasio Somoza García, the longtime dictator of
Nicaragua, before being killed himself

22 TUESDAY

ON THIS DAY 1793
New Year's Day in the French revolutionary calendar,
used from 1793 to 1802

23 WEDNESDAY

24 THURSDAY

ON THIS DAY 1838
A meeting held on Kersal Moor, near Manchester in
England, launches the Chartist movement, the first
mass working-class movement in Europe

25 FRIDAY

ON THIS DAY 1932
Anarchist Catalonia becomes an
'autonomous' region of Spain

26 SATURDAY

ON THIS DAY 1919
Anarchist Nestor Makhno leads his Revolutionary
Insurrectionary Army of Ukraine to an unlikely and
pivotal victory over the vastly superior White Army
in the Russian Civil War

27 SUNDAY

ON THIS DAY 1791
Jews are granted citizenship in revolutionary France

The **SCOTTISH NATIONAL PARTY** overtakes Labour for the first time to become the biggest party in the devolved Scottish Parliament, set up in 1999. The May elections are a turning point in Scottish politics as the SNP forms a minority government with Liberal Democrat and Green support. The Scottish Socialist Party loses all six seats it won in 2003 in the wake of a ruinous split over a defamation case and subsequent perjury charges against its former leader Tommy Sheridan. The SNP goes on to win an overall majority in the 2011 Scottish elections and 50% of the votes and 56 out of 59 seats in the 2015 UK general election. A referendum in 2014 sees a large part of the Scottish left backing independence, but the referendum fails with 55% voting to stay in the UK.

2007

28 MONDAY

Yom Kippur

ON THIS DAY 1864
The International Working Men's Association
(the First International) is founded at a meeting
in St Martin's Hall, London

29 TUESDAY

30 WEDNESDAY

ON THIS DAY 1935
The anti-Stalinist Workers' Party of Marxist
Unification (POUM) is founded in Spain, where
it is especially active during the Civil War

1 THURSDAY

ON THIS DAY 1867
Karl Marx publishes Volume One
of *Das Kapital*

2 FRIDAY

ON THIS DAY 1968
Ten days before the start of the Mexico Olympics,
government troops massacre hundreds of
unarmed protesters at Tlatelolco, Mexico City

3 SATURDAY

Sinead O'Connor rips up a picture of Pope John
Paul II on the US TV programme *Saturday Night
Live* in protest against the Catholic Church's
collusion with child abuse

4 SUNDAY

2008

The world's worst
FINANCIAL CRISIS
for 80 years exposes the global
neoliberal project as little more
than a gigantic economic 'smoke
and mirrors' con-trick. Fears over
risky mortgage lending in the US
have a knock-on effect worldwide
as banks lose confidence in
lending to each other. The
reckless behaviour of a largely
deregulated
banking sector is
epitomised by the collapse of
the Lehman Brothers investment
bank on 15 September. Massive
bailouts are made to financial
institutions as the world
economy slumps into recession.
The price is paid by a new era
of public spending cuts and
austerity.

OCTOBER

5 MONDAY

ON THIS DAY 1789
Tom Paine's *Declaration of the Rights of Man* is published

6 TUESDAY

ON THIS DAY 1536
William Tyndale, translator of the bible into English, is burned at the stake for heresy

7 WEDNESDAY

ON THIS DAY 1979
Landless farmers occupy the Macali estate in Ronda Alta, Brazil, leading to the founding of the Landless Workers' Movement (MST)

8 THURSDAY

ON THIS DAY 1962
The North Korean government announces that a 100% turnout in the Supreme People's Assembly election has resulted in a 100% vote for the Korean People's Party

9 FRIDAY

ON THIS DAY 1967
Revolutionary Marxist and cultural icon Ernesto 'Che' Guevara, who played a major part in the Cuban revolution is captured and summarily executed by CIA-backed Bolivian troops

2009

Barely three years after the withdrawal of its army and 8,500 settlers from **GAZA**, Israel's Operation Cast Lead results in over 1,000 deaths (all but 13 of them Palestinians) in the first of a series of mini-wars during the coming decade. The biggest, the seven-week Operation Protective Edge bombing campaign in 2014, results in more than 2,000 deaths and 10,000 casualties, including many children. Much of the Gazan infrastructure is flattened. Israel justifies the attacks – and its blockade of the territory after the Hamas group seizes power from the Palestinian Authority in 2007 – on security grounds, including rocket attacks and kidnappings organised from Gaza. But a large international solidarity movement develops and attempts are made to break the blockade, including the 'Gaza freedom flotillas', one of which ends with fatalities when Israeli naval commandos storm the *MV Mavi Marmara*.

10 SATURDAY

ON THIS DAY 1911
The Wuchang Uprising begins after the Qing government suppresses protest against the handover of local railways to foreign ventures; the Xinhai Revolution will eventually take down a 2,100-year-old dynastic empire within months

11 SUNDAY

12 MONDAY

Columbus Day
Federal holiday (US)

ON THIS DAY 1995
David McLean, the 'Marlboro Man' who appeared in
advertisements for Marlboro cigarettes from the early
1960s onwards, dies of cancer

13 TUESDAY

ON THIS DAY 1924
UK Labour prime minister Ramsay MacDonald makes
the first party election broadcast on BBC radio

A **CONSERVATIVE-LIBERAL DEMOCRAT COALITION** takes power under David Cameron after the Labour Party loses the general election in May. As well as marking the end of 13 years of New Labour rule, the change of government ushers in a new era of austerity. Chancellor George Osborne's first budget seeks £80 billion 'savings' by 2014/15, requiring departmental spending cuts in most cases of up to 25%. A public sector pay freeze is imposed and, famously, Lib-Dem leader Nick Clegg breaks his election pledge not to introduce university tuition fees. Student protests erupt nationally, helping to radicalise a generation of young people who are already struggling with unprecedented levels of debt.

2010

14 **WEDNESDAY**

15 **THURSDAY**

ON THIS DAY 1968
The Jamaican government bans historian
and activist Walter Rodney from the country,
sparking the Rodney Riots

16 **FRIDAY**

ON THIS DAY 1916
Margaret Sanger opens the first birth control
clinic in New York

17 **SATURDAY**

ON THIS DAY 1961
An estimated 300 Algerian demonstrators,
denouncing France's colonial war in their home
country, are massacred in Paris; the French
government acknowledges 40 victims

18 **SUNDAY**

19 MONDAY

ON THIS DAY 1987
The Guildford Four are released after 15 years in prison, the first of a number of wrongful convictions for IRA bombings that are eventually quashed in the courts

20 TUESDAY

ON THIS DAY 1947
The House Un-American Activities Committee begins its investigation of alleged communists in the US entertainment industry

21 WEDNESDAY

ON THIS DAY 1967
An exorcism and an attempt to 'levitate' the Pentagon add a lighter touch as 100,000 demonstrators assemble in the US capital in the growing protest movement against the Vietnam war

22 THURSDAY

ON THIS DAY 1962
The world comes to the brink of nuclear war as a crisis develops over the placement of Soviet warheads in Fidel Castro's Cuba

23 FRIDAY

ON THIS DAY 1956
Revolution erupts in Hungary; Russian tanks are called in

Starting in Tunisia, where huge demonstrations force hardline president Zine El Abidine Ben to quit and flee to Saudl Arabia, the 'ARAB SPRING' uprisings sweep across north Africa and the Middle East. The millions-strong Tahrir Square protests in Cairo, Egypt, force President Hosni Mubarak from office. Many peaceful pro-democracy protests are brutally suppressed, however, and outright civil war is to envelop Syria, Yemen and Libya, where the long-time dictator Muammar Gaddafi is killed by rebel Islamists in October. In Spain, meanwhile, which has been particularly hard hit by the financial crash, the 'indignados' 15-M (15 May) movement occupies public squares in its battle for social and economic justice. This is followed by the OCCUPY WALL STREET protest in New York in September, which leads to a global Occupy movement with similar protests in almost 1,000 cities in 82 countries.

24 **SATURDAY**

United Nations Day

ON THIS DAY 1945
The UN Charter is ratified by a majority of signatories and the permanent members of the Security Council

25 **SUNDAY**

26 MONDAY

27 TUESDAY

ON THIS DAY 1914
Dylan Thomas born:
'Remember the procession of the old-young men/
From dole queue to corner and back again'

2012

VLADIMIR PUTIN is elected as president of Russia for the third time. Relations with the West slowly sour in the face of an assertive Russian nationalism, while his domestic policies continue the country's increasingly authoritarian and conservative trajectory. A clampdown on dissent is reflected in the jailing of members of the Pussy Riot punk band for 'hooliganism motivated by racial hatred' after they performed an anti-Putin protest song in Moscow's main cathedral. 'We have red lines beyond which starts the destruction of the moral foundations of our society,' Putin declares.

28 WEDNESDAY

ON THIS DAY 1647
The Putney Debates begin, in which members of the
New Model Army, who had recently seized London,
debate Britain's new republican constitution

29 THURSDAY

ON THIS DAY 1929
The Wall Street Crash plunges capitalism
into crisis – again

30 FRIDAY

31 SATURDAY

ON THIS DAY 1517
Martin Luther posts his 95 Theses, sparking
the Reformation

1 SUNDAY

ON THIS DAY 1872
US women's suffrage campaigner Susan B Anthony
and her sisters are arrested for registering to vote

2 MONDAY

ON THIS DAY 1960
A London jury acquits Penguin Books
of obscenity for the publication of *Lady
Chatterley's Lover* by D H Lawrence

3 TUESDAY

ON THIS DAY 1883
The US Supreme Court decides Native
Americans are 'aliens'

4 WEDNESDAY

ON THIS DAY 1780
Quechua leader Tupac Amaru II leads an
indigenous rebellion against Spanish control of
Peru, beginning with the capture and killing of
the Spanish governor by his slave

5 THURSDAY

6 FRIDAY

ON THIS DAY 1990
Forty-seven Saudi women stage a protest against the
country's oppressive gender-segregation regime by
breaking the prohibition on women driving

The United Nations High Commission for Refugees (UNHCR) warns of the worst refugee crisis since the Rwandan genocide in 1994 as 1.8 million people flee the rapidly escalating **SYRIAN CIVIL WAR**. By 2016, half the Syrian population will have been displaced, including five million outside the country. Most of them are in the neighbouring countries of Turkey, Lebanon and Jordan but up to two million will reach Europe. A massive solidarity effort is organised across the continent but it fails to prevent the rise of xenophobic sentiment and support for a 'Fortress Europe' approach to stem the flow. Thousands of refugees will drown in the Mediterranean in the next few years as the overland routes are closed off.

7 SATURDAY

ON THIS DAY 1917
The Bolshevik Revolution is launched and Petrograd seized

8 SUNDAY

ON THIS DAY 1976
Carlos Fonseca, founder of Nicaragua's Sandinista Liberation Front (FSLN), is murdered

9 MONDAY

The Berlin Wall comes down, signalling the
end of the half-century long Cold War

10 TUESDAY

The Nigerian government hangs Ken Saro-Wiwa
and the rest of the Ogoni Nine for their campaigning
against the oil industry, especially Royal Dutch Shell

11 WEDNESDAY

Veterans' Day
Federal holiday (US)

The American slave rebellion leader Nat Turner
is hanged in Jerusalem, Virginia

12 THURSDAY

The father of Irish republicanism Wolfe Tone
commits suicide before execution by the British

13 FRIDAY

14 SATURDAY

Diwali

15 SUNDAY

ON THIS DAY 1988
The 'Palestinian Declaration of
Independence', written by poet
Mahmoud Darwish, is proclaimed

A white police officer's killing of an unarmed black teenager, Michael Brown, in Ferguson, Missouri, sets off nationwide protests under the moniker **BLACK LIVES MATTER**. Now an international movement, Black Lives Matter had started the previous year as a social media hashtag following the acquittal of George Zimmerman for the shooting of black teenager, Trayvon Martin, in Florida. Black Lives Matter brings a new generation of activists to the fore in a campaign against police violence towards black people, and against systemic racism and violence more broadly.

#JUSTICE FOR PHILANDO

2014

NOVEMBER

16 MONDAY

ON THIS DAY 1747
The Knowles Riot in Boston sees hundreds of sailors, labourers and free blacks rise up against British Navy press gangs, temporarily ending impressment

17 TUESDAY

ON THIS DAY 1915
Scottish socialist Mary Barbour leads 'Mrs Barbour's Army' in a rent strike that results in the first rent control act in modern British history

18 WEDNESDAY

ON THIS DAY 1964
After Martin Luther King complains about the FBI's failure to protect civil rights campaigners, FBI director J Edgar Hoover describes him as 'the most notorious liar in the country'

19 THURSDAY

ON THIS DAY 1915
Labour organiser Joe Hill is executed by firing squad at the Utah State Prison

20 FRIDAY

ON THIS DAY 1816
The word 'scab', meaning strikebreaker, is first recorded in print, when it is used by the Albany (New York) Typographical Society

21 SATURDAY

22 SUNDAY

ON THIS DAY 1990
British prime minister Margaret Thatcher resigns

Kurdish fighters break the siege of Kobani, in northern Syria, and turn the tide of war against the so-called **ISLAMIC STATE**, which has seized large swathes of territory in Syria and Iraq and imposed its brutal self-proclaimed 'caliphate' on several million people. Kobani is part of the majority-Kurdish region of north-eastern Syria known as Rojava that established an autonomous administration and militia at the outset of the Syrian civil war. Rojava offers a secular, democratic and egalitarian alternative that inspires many across the world. Its commitment to gender equality and the prominence of women fighters in its ranks marks it out from much of the rest of the region.

2015

23 MONDAY

ON THIS DAY 1170 BCE
The first recorded strike in history involves labourers in the Valley of the Kings necropolis, Egypt, who have not been paid their grain allowance for 20 days

24 TUESDAY

ON THIS DAY 1969
John Lennon returns his MBE to the queen in protest against the wars in Biafra and Vietnam – 'and against Cold Turkey slipping down the charts'

25 WEDNESDAY

ON THIS DAY 1867
Lily Maxwell, a kitchenware shop owner, casts her vote in a Manchester by-election after she is added to the electoral register by mistake ·

26 THURSDAY

Thanksgiving
Federal holiday (US)

ON THIS DAY 1757
'Think in the morning. Act in the noon. Eat in the evening. Sleep in the night.' Happy birthday William Blake

27 FRIDAY

More than 170 world leaders gather at the UN in April to sign the first-ever legally binding climate deal. The deal, agreed at the **PARIS CLIMATE CONFERENCE (COP 21)** at the end of 2015, commits the 195 participating countries to a long-term goal of keeping the global average temperature to 'well below' 2°C above pre-industrial levels. The aim is to keep the increase to 1.5°C in order to mitigate the impacts of dangerous climate change. The agreement is the culmination of many years of campaigning. The US subsequently withdraws following the election of Donald Trump.

2016

SECRETAIRE EXECUTIVE CCNUCC

PRESIDENT

28 SATURDAY

29 SUNDAY

ON THIS DAY 1947
The UN approves the partition of Palestine, despite its rejection by Palestinians and the fact that 90% of privately held land is Arab owned

30 MONDAY

St Andrew's Day
Bank holiday (Scotland)

ON THIS DAY 1999
The World Trade Organisation ministerial meeting in Seattle is disrupted by huge anti-globalisation protests

1 TUESDAY

World Aids Day

ON THIS DAY 1955
Rosa Parks refuses to move to the back of the bus

The **WOMEN'S MARCH ON WASHINGTON**, held the day after Donald Trump's inauguration as US president, turns into the biggest-ever single-day protest in the US. Up to five million people participate in marches across the country, while organisers report a total of 673 marches in 82 countries worldwide. The protests become renowned

2017

for the pink 'pussy hats' worn by many participants in reference to Trump's crude remarks, widely reported during the presidential election, that if he was interested in a woman sexually, 'I don't even wait. And when you're a star, they let you do it. You can do anything. Grab them by the pussy. You can do anything.'

2 WEDNESDAY

ON THIS DAY 1859
Slavery abolitionist John Brown is hanged in Virginia

3 THURSDAY

ON THIS DAY 1984
A gas leak at the Union Carbide pesticide plant in Bhopal, India, kills thousands in the world's worst industrial disaster

4 FRIDAY

5 SATURDAY

ON THIS DAY 1928
The United Fruit Company violently suppresses a workers' strike in Colombia in what becomes known as the Banana Massacre; up to 3,000 are killed

6 SUNDAY

ON THIS DAY 1865
The 13th Amendment is ratified, abolishing slavery in the US

DECEMBER

2018

As the hottest summer on record leads to wildfires across the country, Swedish teenager Greta Thunberg stages a solo protest outside Sweden's parliament to demand climate action. 'I am doing this because you adults are shitting on my future,' her leaflets declare, explaining her refusal to go to school. Her **SCHOOL STRIKE FOR CLIMATE** captures the imagination of school students worldwide and over the coming months hundreds of thousands will stage similar protests in more than 100 countries. Some trade unions also give their backing to climate strikes, while other forms of direct action are growing in the face of the climate emergency.

7 **MONDAY**

8 **TUESDAY**

9 **WEDNESDAY**

ON THIS DAY 1987
Beginning of the First Palestinian Intifada against the
Israeli occupation of the West Bank and Gaza

10 **THURSDAY**

Human Rights Day

ON THIS DAY 1973
US secretary of state Henry Kissinger is awarded the
Nobel Peace Prize, prompting Tom Lehrer to quip that
the award 'made political satire obsolete'

11 **FRIDAY**

12 **SATURDAY**

ON THIS DAY 2005
The COP21 climate summit sees 195 countries
agree to limit the rise in global average temperature
to less than 2°C above pre-industrial levels

13 **SUNDAY**

DECEMBER

14 MONDAY

ON THIS DAY 2008
Iraqi journalist Muntadhar al-Zaidi throws his shoe at US president George W Bush at a press conference

15 TUESDAY

ON THIS DAY 1973
The American Psychiatric Association's Board of Trustees votes to remove homosexuality from its official *Diagnostic and Statistical Manual of Mental Disorders*

2019

The **BREXIT** issue continues to dominate British politics throughout 2019 – and continues to cause problems for the left. While most of the left, including a substantial majority of Labour Party members, are on the Remain side of the argument, they are also highly critical of the EU as an institution and its role in implementing neoliberal policies. A significant left minority opposes UK membership, as it has since the 1970s. Both sides acknowledge the boost Brexit has given to nationalist and xenophobic forces, and the way its dominance of British political debate has diverted focus from the fight against austerity, climate crisis and other issues.

16 WEDNESDAY

ON THIS DAY 1656
Quaker leader James Nayler is arrested for blasphemy
after re-enacting Christ's entry into Jerusalem by
entering Bristol on a donkey

17 THURSDAY

ON THIS DAY 2010
Tunisian street vendor Muhamed Bouazizi's suicide
provokes the first 'Arab Spring' protests

18 FRIDAY

ON THIS DAY 1830
Trials start of almost 2,000 rural labourers who fought
for a minimum wage in England's 'Swing Riots'

19 SATURDAY

20 SUNDAY

21 MONDAY

ON THIS DAY 1907
The Chilean army carries out the Santa Maria School Massacre of striking workers, along with their wives and children; around 3,000 people are murdered

22 TUESDAY

23 WEDNESDAY

ON THIS DAY 1961
James Davis of Livingston, Tennessee, becomes the first of some 58,000 US soldiers killed during the Vietnam War

24 THURSDAY

25 FRIDAY
Christmas Day
Bank/federal holiday (UK and US)

ON THIS DAY 1927
B R Ambedkar, an architect of the Indian constitution born into the Dalit (untouchable) caste, leads followers to burn the *Minusmriti*, an ancient Sanskrit text justifying the caste hierarchy

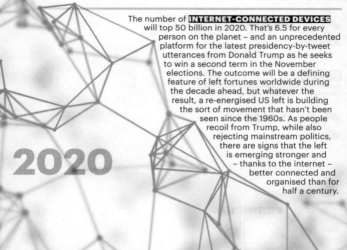

The number of **INTERNET-CONNECTED DEVICES** will top 50 billion in 2020. That's 6.5 for every person on the planet – and an unprecedented platform for the latest presidency-by-tweet utterances from Donald Trump as he seeks to win a second term in the November elections. The outcome will be a defining feature of left fortunes worldwide during the decade ahead, but whatever the result, a re-energised US left is building the sort of movement that hasn't been seen since the 1960s. As people recoil from Trump, while also rejecting mainstream politics, there are signs that the left is emerging stronger and – thanks to the internet – better connected and organised than for half a century.

2020

26 SATURDAY

Boxing Day

ON THIS DAY 1492
The first Spanish colony in the New World is founded by Christopher Columbus at La Navidad (modern-day Môle-Saint-Nicolas, in Haiti)

27 SUNDAY

ON THIS DAY 1831
Charles Darwin sets sail from England on *HMS Beagle* on a journey that will eventually lead to his theory of evolution and the origin of species

28 MONDAY

Boxing Day

ON THIS DAY 1793
Tom Paine is arrested by Robespierre as the French
Revolutionary Terror reaches its height

29 TUESDAY

30 WEDNESDAY

ON THIS DAY 1884
William Morris, Eleanor Marx and others
establish the Socialist League

31 THURSDAY

ON THIS DAY 1967
The Youth International Party, the Yippies, is formed
at Abbie Hoffman's New York home

1 FRIDAY

New Year's Day
Bank/federal holiday (UK and US)